思い出のサダコ
Memories of Sadako

大倉記代=著
宮本慶子=訳
スティーブン・リーパー=監訳
夜川けんたろう=絵

IBCパブリッシング

Text ©Kiyo Okura 2005
English text ©Keiko Miyamoto 2010
Illustrations ©Kentarou Yokawa 2010
Translation supervised by Steven Lloyd Leeper
©Yomo Publishing Ltd. 2010
(Hase 5-11-21 #202, Kamakura City, Kanagawa Prefecture, 248-0016, Japan)
©IBC Publishing, Inc. 2015

Published by IBC Publishing, Inc.
29-3 Nakazato-cho
Shinjuku-ku, Tokyo 162-0804
www.ibcpub.co.jp

All rights reserved. No part of this book may be reproduced
in any form without written permission from the publisher.

First Edition 2015

ISBN978-4-7946-0353-1
Printed in Japan

Three Months with Sadako at the Doorway to Adolescence

思春期の入り口にいた三か月

Translation supervised by Steven Lloyd Leeper
監訳：スティーブン・ロイド・リーパー

Translation by Keiko Miyamoto
訳：宮本 慶子

Illustrated by Kentarou Yokawa
絵：夜川 けんたろう

This translation is dedicated to my friends
Kiyo, Michiko and Atsuko
Hoping for lasting world peace with no nuclear weapons
and NO MORE SADAKOS!

Keiko Miyamoto

Special thanks to

Michiko Pumpian, Hidetaka Takizawa

Elizabeth Baldwin

Naoko Kondo

Yoko Nakazawa, Mutsuko Ohikata

Dave Feickert (New Zealand)

Rosalie Huzzard (UK)

Wendy L. Geiger, Ph.D (USA)

Masayuki Murata (Hanshichi Printing co., Ltd.)

Ken Matsumura (august design Inc.)

Preface

The Story of Sadako Sasaki

Sadako was one step away from becoming a young woman when she died.

On August 6, 1945, an atomic bomb was detonated above Hiroshima, the first time for a nuclear weapon to be used against human beings. The country that dropped the bomb was the United States, with which Japan had been at war for four years.

At 8:15 AM there was a flash in the sky, and instantly tens of thousands of people lost their lives. Until then, no one knew that atomic bombs possessed such devastating power.

The sky above was a pure blue, and then a blinding blaze of light illuminated everything under it. Minutes later all living creatures were plummeted into an unearthly hell. People

まえがき

思春期の入り口に立ったサダコちゃん

　サダコは、これから思春期に入るかというときに亡くなったのでした。
　1945年8月6日、人類初の核兵器原子爆弾が広島の上空で炸裂しました。飛行機から爆弾を落としたのは日本と4年間戦争を続けていたアメリカ合衆国です。

　午前8時15分、ピカッと光った原爆は一瞬にして何万人もの命を奪える力を持った爆弾です。その恐ろしい力がどれほどのものであるのか、この時までまだ誰にもわかっていませんでした。
　真っ青の夏の空が一瞬の眩いひかりによってカーッと照らされたあと、地上にいた人々は数分の後に地獄へと導かれたのです。路上に出ていた人は一瞬のうちに全身くろこげになって即死したり、まっ

above ground were instantly transformed into char and died immediately, or had their bright-red skin melt on their bodies, writhing in pain as they wandered about begging for water. Hiroshima had become a scene from hell.

At this time Sadako Sasaki, who would later become known throughout the world as a symbol of the young lives lost to the bomb, was two years old. She was being held in the arms of her mother. And then rain fell—black rain—filled with radioactivity.

Sadako, however, suffered no outward injuries. When she entered elementary school, she was an active child and a fast runner. She joined the relay team and was as good as the boys. She did her best at everything she tried, and she was popular among her classmates.

But then, as the last winter of her elementary school years approached, Sadako began to feel unwell and ended up visiting the hospital. It was there she learned that the cause was

かに焼け爛れた皮膚の痛みにうめきながら水を求めて歩き回ったり、広島はまさに地獄絵のようになりました。

　この時、後に「サダコ」として世界中の人に知られるようになる佐々木禎子さんは２歳。お母さんの腕に抱かれていました。そして雨にあたったのです。後に「黒い雨」と呼ばれる放射能を含んだ雨です。

　でも禎子ちゃんは無傷でしたし、小学校にあがっても足の速い活発な少女としてすくすく育っていきました。学校ではリレーの選手。男の子にも負けません。なんでもがんばりやの禎子ちゃんはクラスでも人気者でした。

　ところが秋の運動会が終わり、小学校最後の冬を迎えたあたりから禎子ちゃんの体の具合が悪くなり、とうとう病院にいくことになりました。そしてそれが10年前の原爆で受けた放射能のせいである

the radioactivity she had been exposed to 10 years earlier in Hiroshima. Just before she was supposed to enter junior high school, she was hospitalized at the Hiroshima Red Cross Hospital.

The black rain that had fallen on her when she was two was causing havoc to her body. She wouldn't be able to attend the elementary school graduation ceremony, and she wouldn't be able to take part in the matriculation ceremony for junior high school students.

The popular Sadako's hospitalization caused a great deal of concern among her classmates, but when they went to visit her, she was bright and cheerful. While she wasn't entirely ignorant of the cause of her illness, she soon became friends with the other patients and went cheerfully around the ward wearing a dress, not a hospital gown.

In June Sadako was moved into a two-patient room, which she would share with Kiyo Okura, who was two years older.

ことがわかり、中学校進学を目前にして広島赤十字病院に入院しました。

　２歳の時にお母さんの腕の中で受けた雨、「黒い雨」が禎子ちゃんの体の中で暴れ始めたのです。小学校の卒業式も出られず、中学校の入学式にも出られませんでした。

　同級生たちは人気者の禎子ちゃんの突然の入院に驚き、心配しました。でも禎子ちゃんは同級生がお見舞いにくると明るく明るくふるまっていました。自分の病気がなんであるのか、まったく知らないわけではなかったのですが、禎子ちゃんは同じ病棟の患者さんたちともすぐ仲良くなり、寝巻きを着ないでワンピース姿で病院中をとびはねていたのです。
　この年の６月、禎子ちゃんは２人部屋の病室にかわりました。ここで２歳年上の大倉記代さんに出会うのです。禎子ちゃん12歳、記

Sadako was then twelve, Kiyo fourteen. Kiyo made Sadako feel at home, and for the next three months the two of them folded paper cranes side by side in the hope of getting better. This was a very special time for Sadako.

    Until near the end of her life, Kiyo didn't speak much of the three months spent with Sadako. She devoted most of her time to activities opposing nuclear weapons. But in 2005, after attending the international meeting on Nuclear Non-proliferation in New York, she learned that she had cancer. With the time left her, she wanted to do one more thing. Through Sadako she wanted to tell the world about the horror of nuclear weapons that took innocent young lives. The result is this book.

    May, 2015

                                   Setsuko Yokokawa
                                   Yomo Publishing Ltd.

代さん14歳。まさに思春期の入り口に立った禎子ちゃんを2歳お姉さんの記代さんはやさしく迎えてくれました。8月末に記代さんが退院するまで2人はベッドを並べて、病気が治ることを願いながら鶴を折り続けました。禎子ちゃんにとって素晴らしい時となったのです。

　その3か月間の想い出を記代さんは晩年になるまで多くは語ってきませんでした。ただひたすら核兵器反対の運動を続けてきた記代さんでしたが、2005年にニューヨークで開かれた核不拡散条約の世界大会に出席して帰国した直後にガンであることがわかりました。大倉さんはどうしても書き残しておきたい、若い命を奪う原爆がどれほど恐ろしいものであるかをサダコちゃんの姿を通して今こそ世界中の人々に知ってほしい、と筆をとりました。それが本書です。

　2015年5月

よも出版 代表
横川 節子

Contents

Preface　まえがき ……………………………………… 6

Chapter 1　**The First Encounter**
出会い ……………………………………………… 17

Chapter 2　**An Idol**
アイドル …………………………………………… 29

Chapter 3　**Hospital as Playground**
病院中が遊び場だった …………………………… 35

Chapter 4　**Yuki's Death**
ゆきちゃんの死 …………………………………… 45

Chapter 5　**Never Again the Atomic Bomb**
原爆を許すまじ …………………………………… 51

Chapter 6　**One Thousand Paper Cranes**
千羽鶴 ……………………………………………… 61

Chapter 7　**Entering Adolescence**
思春期の入り口に立つ …………………………… 73

Chapter 8　**To the Starry Heavens**
星空へ ……………………………………………… 85

Epilogue　その後 ……………………………………………… 92
Afterword　あとがき ……………………………………………… 102
Sadako and Kiyo　禎子ちゃんと記代さん ……………………… 106
About Sadako　禎子ちゃんについて …………………………… 112
About Kiyo Okura　大倉記代さんについて …………………… 118
Sadako In the World　世界中で愛されるサダコ ……………… 122

Chapter 1

The First Encounter
出会い

| Chapter 1

I met Sadako Sasaki for the first time in June 1955 at the Hiroshima Red Cross Hospital. It was strange that we had not encountered each other before. I had been in the hospital since December 1954 with pulmonary infiltration (an early stage of tuberculosis), and Sadako was suddenly admitted just two months later. We had both been assigned to the rather small Pediatrics & Gynecology Ward, yet we never found each other until June.

This may be because wintertime was perfect for lolling around in my cozy bed, losing myself in my favorite books. My hospital bed had become the perfect sanctuary for my favorite pastime: reading. Hospitalized at the age of 14, I was the oldest patient in the children's ward. Most of the others were preschool children. I was always placed in a room with gynecology patients. With children coming in and out of our room, I gradually became close to their mothers.

Word

- **Red Cross Hospital**　赤十字病院
- **encounter**　動 出会う
- **pulmonary infiltration**　肺浸潤
- **tuberculosis**　名 結核
- **pediatrics**　名 小児科
- **gynecology**　名 婦人科
- **ward**　名 病棟
- **sanctuary**　名 聖域

The First Encounter　出会い

　私が禎子ちゃんと出会ったのは昭和30年6月、広島日赤病院でした。禎子ちゃんはこの年2月に緊急入院をし、私はその前年の12月から肺浸潤で入院していたのに、たいして広くもない小児科・婦人科病棟でウソのように出会うことがなかったのです。

　原因は多分、横着者の私にとって寒い間暖かいふとんに寝転がって本が好きなだけ読める、こんな幸せなことはなく病院内のことにあまり関心がなかったからでしょう。14歳で入院した私は、小児科病棟では最年長。あとは就学前の子どもたちばかりのようで、二人部屋の相方はいつも婦人科の方でした。

| Chapter 1

Around me were nurses, cleaning ladies and meal servers, so I heard plenty about what was happening in the hospital. I remember someone mentioning that a girl my age had been admitted, but such things failed to arouse my curiosity. I was too focused on myself to think about others. Passing through adolescence, I was bewildered by my own mental and physical changes. Unconcerned with my surroundings, I was only interested in my emotional and intellectual development. My friends and I would talk about my inner confusion.

Before coming to the hospital, school was everything to me. I'm not talking about my schoolwork, of course, but the best friends with whom I spent every second of my day. That's why I didn't notice my disease progressing. These days, children use cell phones to socialize by mailing or texting with

Word

- **arouse** 動 (感情などを) 刺激する
- **curiosity** 名 好奇心
- **adolescence** 名 思春期
- **bewilder** 動 ～を当惑させる
- **intellectual** 形 知性の
- **progress** 動 進行する

The First Encounter　出会い

　小さな子どもたちが出入りし、いつの間にかそのお母さんとも親しくなり、その他に看護婦さん、掃除や配膳(はいぜん)をして下さるおばさんたち、と大人に囲まれているのでベッド生活だけの私にも病院内のいろんなことが耳に入ってきます。同じような年の子が入ってきたよ、とは聞いていましたが、とりたてて好奇心をかきたてられることはありませんでした。当時思春期に入っていた私は自分の心と体の変化に戸惑(とまど)い、まわりのことにはあまり目がいかなかったのです。関心があるのは、自分の内面の変化とそれを語り合える友人たちでした。

　病気の進行にも気がつかないくらい学校が楽しくて楽しくて……もちろん勉強なんてことはありません。今でいうとケイタイ友達なのでしょうか、毎日会っているのに、手紙など書きあって、今何を読んでいる、とか映画俳優、特に洋画の誰がどうだとか、ちょっと背伸びした内面の打ち明け話は日々の糧(かて)のように重要でした。

Chapter 1

their peers. My friends and I just hung out together, sharing everyday nonsense or talking about the foreign movie stars that attracted our attention. We found joy in every corner of teenage life and shared the growing pains we each shouldered separately.

Those talks were my fuel, my energy. My sudden hospitalization cut them off. To alleviate my lonely despair, I spent hours writing letters and keeping up with my diary. I was never bored.

Sadako was transferred to my room after a previous roommate was discharged. She entered the room shyly, escorted by a nurse, holding tightly to a parcel of clothing.

She looked nervous, probably because she was losing a familiar room and coming to a new environment.

Word
- **peer** 名 友人
- **fuel** 名 燃料
- **alleviate** 動 (苦しみなどを) 和らげる
- **transfer** 動 移動させる
- **previous** 形 以前の
- **discharge** 動 退院させる

それを突然中断され、一人隔離(かくり)されたことは人生初の絶望でした。それを埋めるために、手紙や日記を書くことにもたくさんの時間を使い、退屈などということはなかったのです。

　隣りの婦人科の方が退院されたのをきっかけに禎子ちゃんが私の部屋に移ってきました。

　着替えの小さな風呂敷(ふろしき)包みを抱え、婦長さんに付き添われて現れた禎子ちゃんの顔は少し緊張していました。

| Chapter 1

Sadako was extremely meticulous and careful about details. While pajamas suited me just fine, she changed into a white blouse and skirt every morning, neatly folding her clothes in the evening.

Every morning, she astonished me by braiding her own hair. At home, my mother always braided my hair when I was 12. Sadako was only 12. I thought she was too young to behave that way or even know how. She was mature for her age. At least that's what I thought.

Knowing we felt awkward, the nurse introduced us with a smile. "Kiyo-san, this is Sasaki Sadako-chan. Sadako-chan, this is Okura Kiyo-san. She's two years older than you. Kiyo-san, please look after her, okay?"

Word

- **meticulous** 形 とても几帳面な
- **neatly** 副 きちんと
- **astonish** 動 (人を)驚かせる
- **braid** 動 (髪などを)編む
- **mature** 形 大人っぽい
- **awkward** 形 居心地が悪い
- **look after** ～の面倒を見る

きまじめそうな印象に、入院でますますズボラになっている私としてはちょっとたじろぐ思いがありました。案にたがわず、禎子ちゃんはとても几帳面で、寝まきを着たまま一日を過ごす私とちがい、朝起きるとブラウスとスカートに着替え、脱いだものはキチンとたたんでいました。

　三つ編みの髪も、毎朝一人で整えるのです。同じ六年生の頃、朝ごはんを食べながら母に三つ編みをしてもらっていた私は、ただただ目をみはるばかりでした。

　固くなっている二人を、婦長さんが「佐々木禎子ちゃんよ、よろしくね。こちらは大倉記代さん、二つお姉さんだから、よろしくね」と両方の肩に手を置いて紹介してくれました。

Chapter 1

After an awkward silence, we greeted each other. She started putting away her clothes. Just then, I noticed a shaft of light entering our room.

The moment Sadako saw it, she grabbed her hand mirror and dashed out. I had no idea what was going on. I looked out of the window and saw that this was how she signaled "hello" to a friend on the other side of the building.

Our room faced north, so the sun didn't shine directly in. Sadako had rushed back to her old room, which faced east toward the morning sun. From there she flashed "hello" to her friend with her mirror. As you can imagine, this event broke the ice between us.

Word

- **put away** 片付ける
- **shaft** 名 一筋の光
- **grab** 動 つかみ取る
- **have no idea** 全くわからない
- **go on** （出来事などが）起こる
- **face** 動 （ある方向に）面する
- **break the ice** 緊張をほぐす

お互いぎこちなく挨拶を交わして彼女が自分の荷物を開き始めた時、キラッと一つの光の球が飛び込んできました。

　それを察知した瞬間、禎子ちゃんは傍らの手鏡を持ってパーっと部屋を飛び出していったのです。私は一瞬あっけにとられましたが、それでもその光の原因がわかったので窓の外を覗くと案の定、二つの光の球は攻防戦を繰り広げていました私たちの部屋は北向きで陽が当たりません。

　中庭を挟んだ向かいの部屋の患者さんが禎子ちゃんの引っ越しに挨拶を送ってきたので、禎子ちゃんは東向きで午前中は陽が当たる古巣の大部屋に帰り、そこから返事を返していたのです。これで初対面の緊張が解けたのは言うまでもありません。

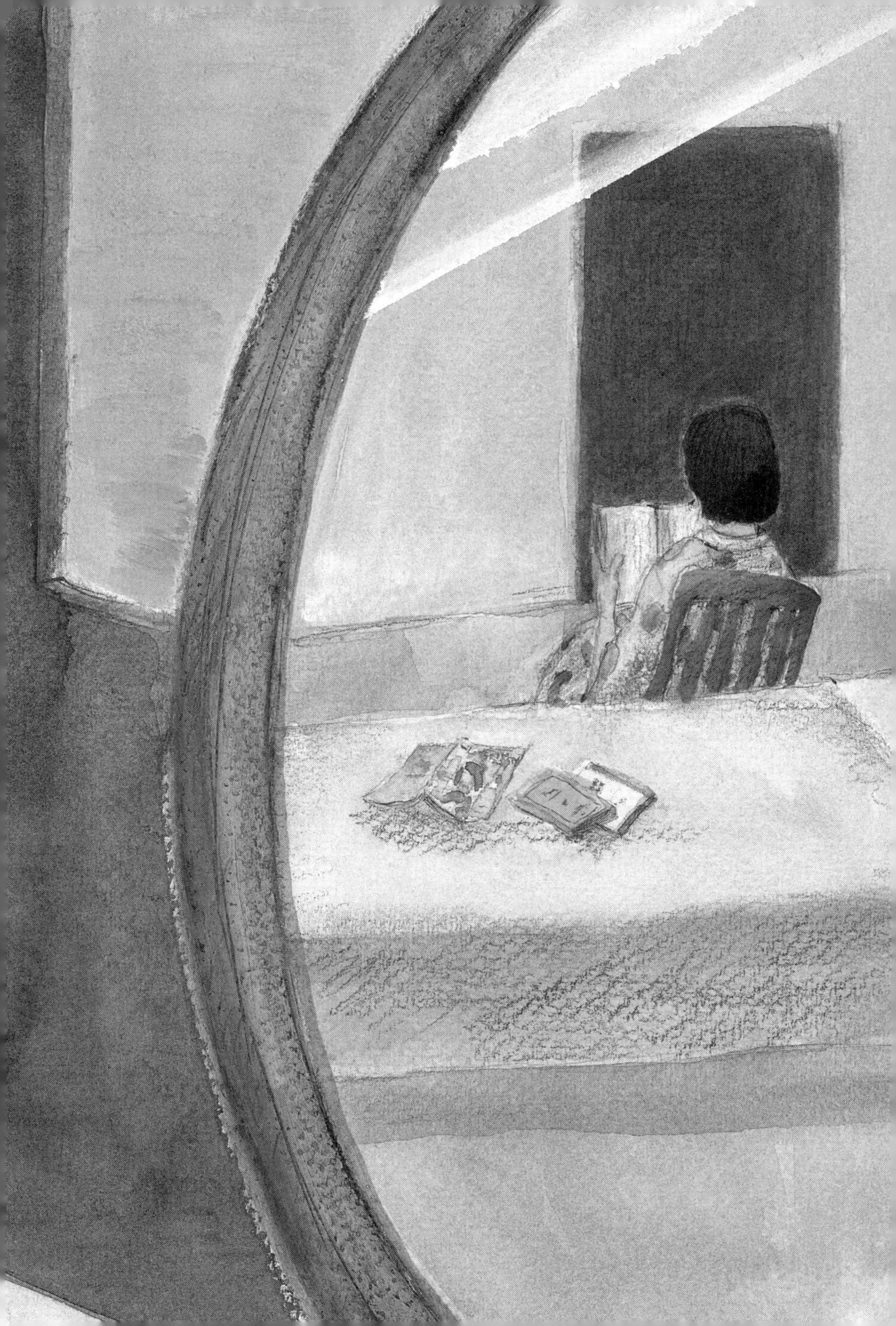

Chapter 2

An Idol

アイドル

Sadako was more popular than I ever wanted to be. Although we were in a big hospital, everybody knew her and she knew everyone. Even though I had been in the hospital longer, she had made more friends. She befriended anyone she met: child patients, their mothers, internal and surgical patients, nurses, cleaning ladies, and even kitchen staff. Her uniquely magnetic personality attracted all who encountered her. She was an *idol* wherever she popped up.

Sadako's symptoms, which had been serious enough to require immediate hospitalization, became stable thanks to intensive care. She must have given up on becoming a junior high school student, but she always looked so vibrant. I believe that her phenomenal energy was what repelled her disease for a time. Her spirit lived to the fullest, like a candle burning intensely just before it goes out. For those three months she

Word

- **surgical** 形 外科の
- **magnetic** 形 人を引きつける
- **pop up** 不意に現れる
- **symptom** 名 症状
- **require** 動 ～を必要とする
- **stable** 形 安定した
- **vibrant** 形 活力のある
- **phenomenal** 形 驚異的な
- **repel** 動 ～をはねのける
- **intensely** 副 猛烈に

An Idol アイドル

　話を聞けば聞くほど、どちらが先輩かわからないくらい彼女は病院中の人と友だちになっていました。子どもたちとそのお母さん。内科、外科の患者さんと、そこの看護婦さん、配膳やお掃除など雑用をして下さるおばさんたち。とにかく入院病棟で禎子ちゃんを知らない人はいなかったのではないでしょうか。今でいうアイドルだったのだと思います。

　緊急入院するくらい悪かった症状も集中治療で安定し、それでも中学校には行けないあきらめを通り過ぎると、ちょうど蝋燭の火が燃え尽きる一瞬、大きく輝くと言われるように私が一緒だった3か月彼女は夏に向かう陽射しのように明るく輝いていました。

| Chapter 2

was—to everyone, but especially to me—a shining light in the sky or the sunshine of early summer.

    I sometimes saw her getting blood transfusions. I knew that she had been copying her weekly blood test results, but I didn't know her disease was so serious. Sadako enjoyed walking around the hospital, so she often didn't come back to our room to have her temperature taken. It was clever of her to take her temperature in other friends' wards.

Word

☐ **blood transfusion** 輸血   ☐ **temperature** 名 体温
☐ **copy** 動 写しを取る

An Idol　アイドル

　時に輸血をする姿も見ていたのに、血液検査の結果をメモしていたことも知っていたのに、私にはその深刻さより検温時間にも帰ってこないでよその病棟で済ませてしまうくらい病院生活を楽しんでいた彼女の方が印象に残っています。そこは子ども、内からあふれる生命力は束の間、病をも退ける勢いだったのでしょうか。

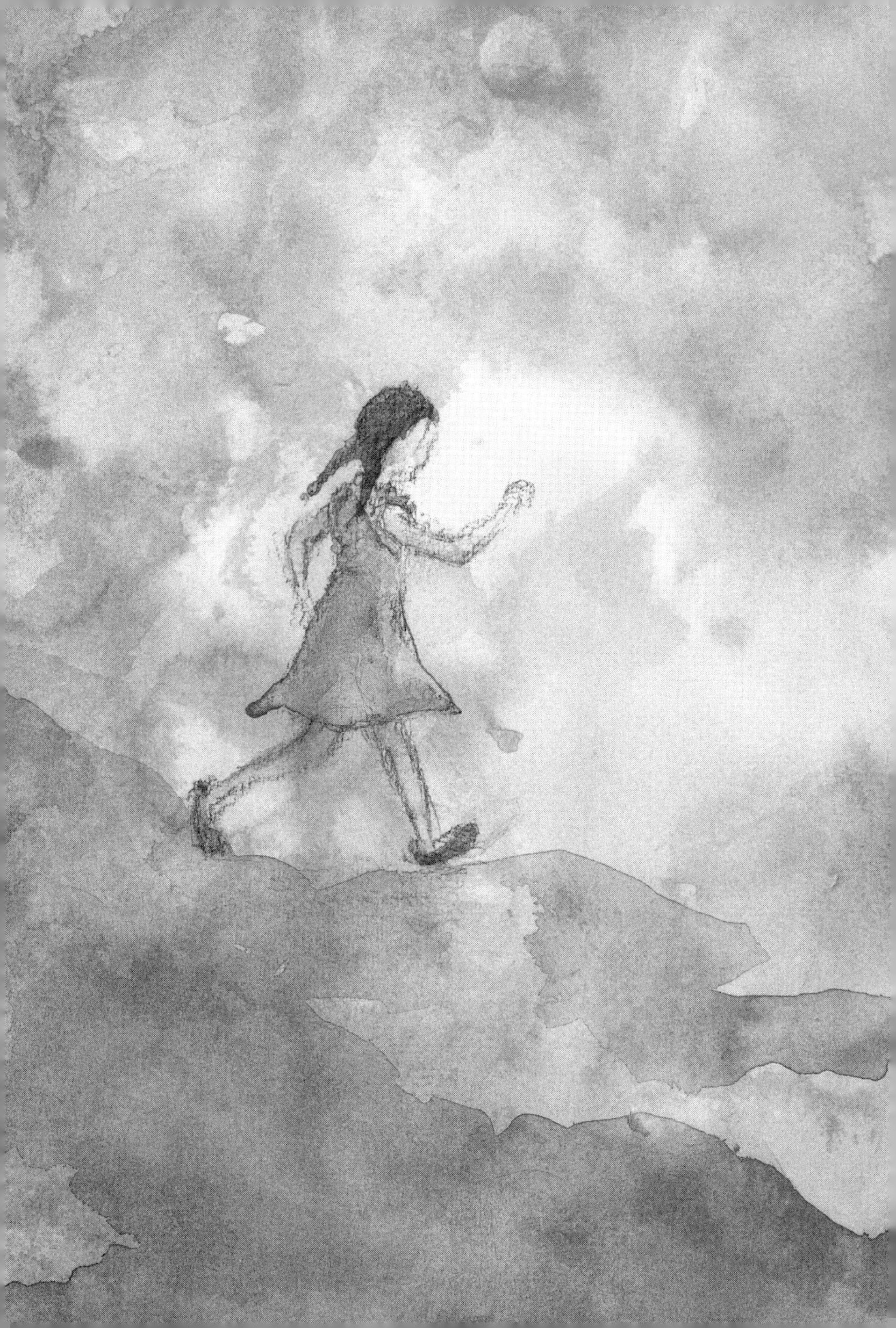

Chapter 3

Hospital as Playground
病院中が遊び場だった

| Chapter 3

Even becoming Sadako's roommate failed to awaken my interest in hospital doings. I would rather read my books and write letters to my friends. In contrast, after breakfast and the taking of her temperature, Sadako busily collected news in the Internal Medicine and Surgical wards to share with me. This was her routine.

One day, Sadako introduced me to a young, beautiful lady who was visiting a patient. Later, that lady came to our hospital as a nutritionist in training. She asked us if there was something we particularly wanted to eat. She told us she could make a special request because it was her final week of training. Then, she ordered our favorite foods, and we had a special treat.

Word

- **in contrast**　対照的に
- **collect**　動 収集する
- **internal medicine**　内科
- **routine**　名 日課
- **nutritionist**　名 栄養士
- **treat**　名 ごちそう

一緒の部屋になったものの、私は相変わらず友人との文通と読書に明け暮れ、病院内のことにはあまり関心がありませんでした。その点禎子ちゃんは行動的で、日課のように、朝食後の検温が済むと内科、外科の病棟へ出かけてはいろんな情報を持ち込んでくれました。

　ある時、きれいなお姉さんを紹介してくれました。内科の患者さんのお見舞い客だった人で、後に栄養士の実習に来られ、最後の週には、「献立に自由がきくからあなたたちの食べたい物言って」とリクエストを出させて下さいました。

Chapter 3

Another day, Sadako suggested that we eat boiled cabbage. During those days, people attending patients could cook in the hospital. Sadako and I went out to buy a cabbage. Sometimes hospital food tasted so bland; even a simple boiled cabbage with bonito flakes and a little soy sauce was a treat. The cabbage we cooked definitely enlivened our simple hospital meals.

Sadako knew that I'd written *tanka* (short Japanese poems of 31 syllables) and other poetry. After visiting a patient who could appreciate my poems, she took me to the Internal Medicine Ward to introduce me to him.

Kids in the hospital loved Sadako because she was so much fun to play with. Around her, the sound of laughter echoed through wards.

Word

- suggest 動 ～を提案する
- bland 形 味気ない
- bonito flake 鰹節
- soy sauce 醤油
- definitely 副 間違いなく
- enliven 動 ～を活気づける
- syllable 名 音節
- appreciate 動 ～を活気づける
- laughter 名 笑い声
- echo 動 こだまする

またある時はキャベツをゆでておかずにしようと言うのです。当時、付き添いの家族は自炊(じすい)も可能でした。どこかでそれを見てきて早速やってみようと二人でキャベツを買いに行きました。鰹節と醬油だけの味つけでしたが、ものたりない病院の食事に彩りを添えました。

　私が詩や短歌を書いているのを知って、それを見てくれるという人を訪ね内科の病室にも連れて行ってくれました。

　子どもたちは相手をしてくれる禎子ちゃんが好きで、その周(まわ)りにはいつも笑い声が聞こえていました。

| Chapter 3

One day, a group of kids came running into our room with Sadako. She wanted to show me a funny kid. The boy couldn't pronounce "*hako*" (box) correctly. I pointed to a box and asked him many times, "What's this?"

He answered, "*hato*" (dove).

Sadako began carefully and seriously teaching him how to pronounce "*hako*." "Say '*ha*.'"

The boy repeated, "*ha*."

Sadako said, "*ko*."

"*ko*."

Word
- **pronounce** 動 発音する
- **correctly** 副 正確に
- **point** 動 指さす
- **dove** 名 ハト

ある時、その集団が私たちの部屋へ走りこんできたのです。一人の子がどうしても箱のことを「ハト」としか発音できないというのがおかしいと、私の前で再現してくれるというのです。たしかにその小さな子は箱を示して「これ何？」と何度きいてもハトとしか言えません。

　禎子ちゃんはむきになって、「一言ずつ区切って『は』って言ってごらん」

　「ハッ」

　「こ」

　「コッ」

Chapter 3

"Now say, '*hako*.'"

The kid said, "*hato*!"

Looking back, I understood that he was putting us on. At that time, I just laughed out loud.

Word

☐ **put someone on** （人を）からかう　　☐ **laugh out loud** 大笑いする

「じゃあ『はこ』」

「ハト！」

　思えば、私たちはその小さな子に遊ばれていたのですが、当時は二人の対照的なやり取りにただただ笑い転げたものでした。

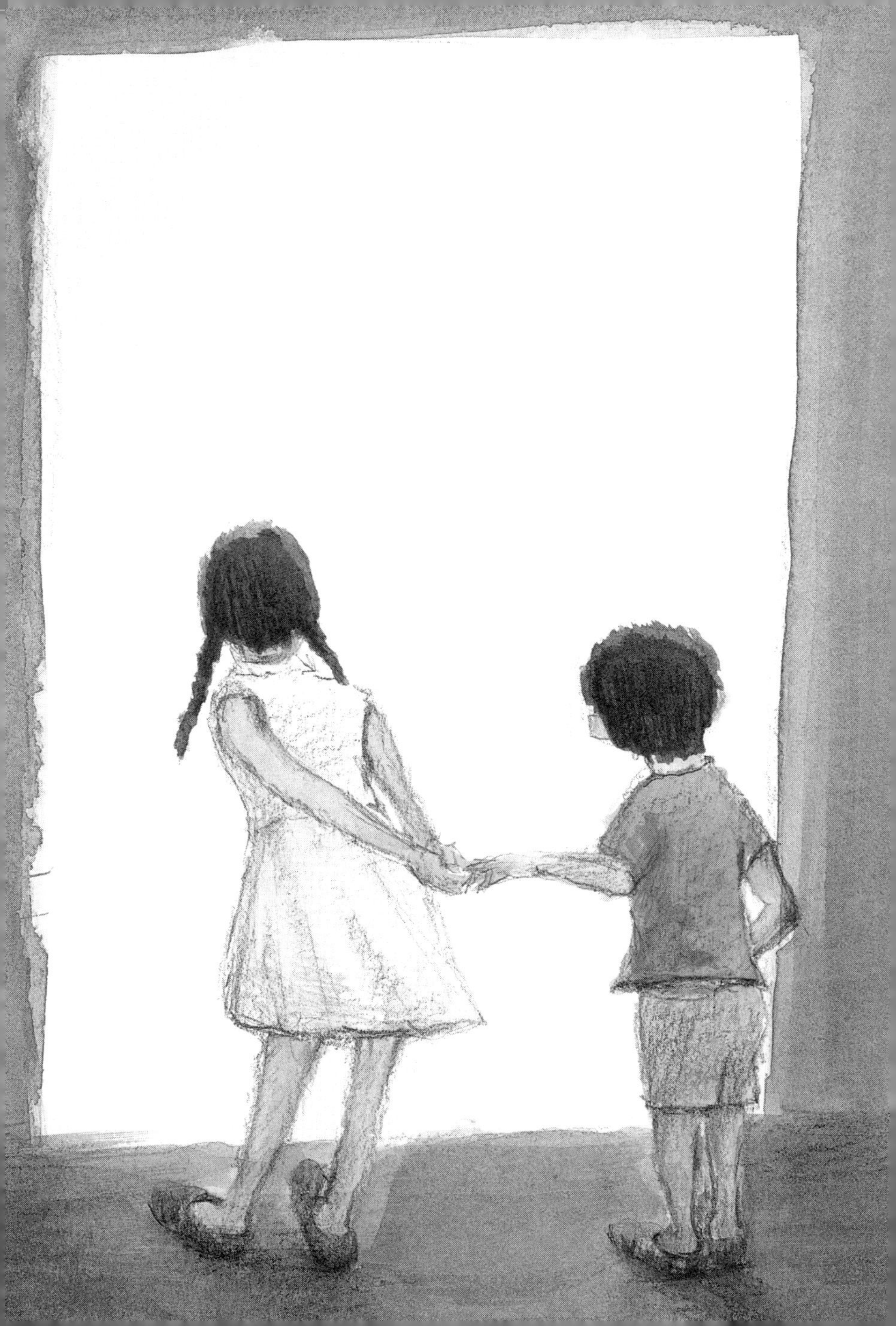

Chapter 4

Yuki's Death
ゆきちゃんの死

| *Chapter 4*

In the middle of rainy season, a cute little girl named Yuki died of acute leukemia. She was about five years old, with snowy white skin like a china doll. We saw her only when her mom walked the hallways carrying her on her back. (Yuki seemed to have passed the heavy legs stage; her anemia had progressed to the point that her legs truly hurt). Whenever they passed us in a long hallway, we said, "Hi." She could only respond with a weak, wan smile.

We never played with her like we did with other kids.

One day, Yuki's mom came to us to say, "Would you please say a last good-bye to Yuki?"

We walked down the steps to the morgue in the basement to offer incense for the repose of a departed soul.

Word

- **acute leukemia**　急性白血病
- **china**　形 陶磁器の
- **hallway**　名 廊下
- **anemia**　名 貧血
- **wan**　形 青白い
- **morgue**　名 霊安室
- **offer incense**　焼香する
- **repose**　名 安らぎ
- **departed**　形 亡くなった

Yuki's Death　ゆきちゃんの死

　梅雨のさなか、ゆきちゃんという、5歳ぐらいの色白で、お人形のように可愛い女の子が急性白血病で亡くなるということがありました。
　私たちは、お母さんに背負われて（貧血が進むと足がだるいのを通りこして、痛くて歩けないのだそうです）散歩している姿を何度か見かけ声をかけると弱々しい笑顔を返してくるだけで、他の子供たちのように一緒に遊んだことはありませんでした。

　それでもお母さんに「最後のお別れをしてやってくださいませんか」と言われ、二人して地下の霊安室に焼香に行きました。

| Chapter 4

Purple (subcutaneous hemorrhage) spots were visible not only on her arms and legs but also on her fair-skinned face. Aghast and petrified by the cruelty of her death, we held our breath.

We offered incense. We were walking silently to our room when Sadako suddenly asked, "Am I going to die like her?"

I gasped. Now I knew for sure that Sadako knew what disease she had. "Never say such a stupid thing!" Spontaneously, I hugged her shoulders.

Under her *yukata* (thin cotton kimono) her shoulders were much thinner than I had expected. I can't forget the feel of those skinny, weak shoulders. On that chilly rainy night, we hugged each other and cried. It was the first time that I felt I looked straight at Sadako.

Word

- **subcutaneous** 形 皮下の
- **hemorrhage** 名 出血
- **aghast** 形 がくぜんとして
- **petrified** 形 驚き立ちすくんで
- **cruelty** 名 残酷さ
- **spontaneously** 副 無意識のうちに
- **chilly** 形 肌寒い

Yuki's Death　ゆきちゃんの死

　手足だけでなく、人形のように色白だった顔にもはっきりと紫斑(しはん)が表れそのむごい姿に私たちは一瞬ハッと息を呑み、立ちすくんでしまいました。

　焼香を終え、無言で病室に帰る途中、突然禎子ちゃんが「ウチもああなって死ぬんじゃろうか」とポツンと言いました。

　私はハッとして、ああこの子は自分の病気を知っていると思いました。「バカ言んさんな」と思わず肩を抱いたのですが、薄い浴衣(ゆかた)に包まれた彼女の肩は想像以上にやせて骨ばっていて、その感触は今も忘れられません。
　雨の肌寒い夜、薄暗い廊下で二人抱き合って泣きました。この時初めて、私は禎子ちゃんの方を見た気がします。

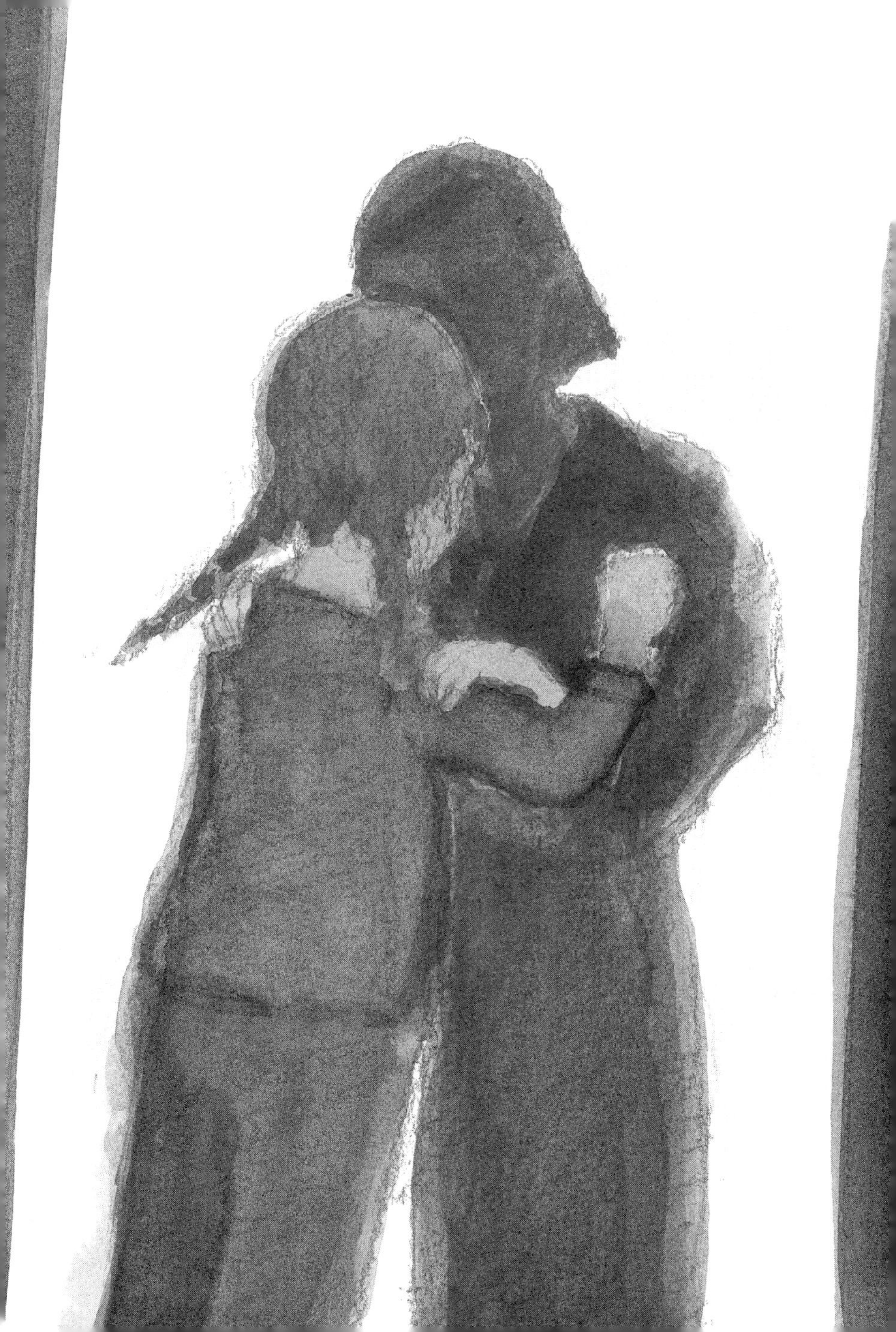

Chapter 5

Never Again
the Atomic Bomb

原爆を許すまじ

| Chapter 5

Sadako taught me a song called *Never Again the Atomic Bomb*. One day in August 1955, she told me she heard someone say, "A Chinese delegation's coming today!" I followed Sadako up to a third-floor lecture room, but we weren't allowed to enter. We listened to the song through the closed door.

At the time, I had no clue what that delegation was. I had never even heard of the First World Conference against Atomic and Hydrogen Bombs, which was held that year. Sadako and I were simply attracted to the singing we heard in the hallway.

A couple of days later, on August 5th, Sadako left to spend a few days at home.

Word

- **never again**　二度と（〜ない）
- **atomic bomb**　原子爆弾
- **delegation**　名 代表団
- **clue**　名 ヒント
- **conference**　名 協議大会
- **hydrogen bomb**　水素爆弾

「原爆を許すまじ」の歌を教えてくれたのも禎子ちゃんでした。8月に入ったある日「今日中国の代表団が来る」という情報を仕入れてきた禎子ちゃんについて3階の講堂まで見に行きましたが中に入ることはできず、閉まった扉の外で耳を傾けただけでした。

　当時は何の代表団か、ましてその年が第一回原水爆禁止世界大会だったことなど知るよしもなく、ただ漏れてきた歌声に心惹かれました。

　その2、3日後、8月5日、禎子ちゃんは外泊しました。

| Chapter 5

On August 6th, Sadako and her family went to the Peace Memorial Park to attend the 10th Hiroshima Peace Memorial Ceremony. All of a sudden, she began bleeding from the gums. They immediately brought her back to the hospital.

To my surprise, Sadako said, "Overnight, I memorized *Never Again the Atomic Bomb*." She knew the melody and all the lyrics and taught them to me.

This song, which I have been singing ever since, dates back to that day for me.

Word

- **bleed** 動 出血する
- **gum** 名 歯茎
- **memorize** 動 〜を丸暗記する
- **lyric** 名 歌詞
- **ever since** その後ずっと
- **date back to** 〜にさかのぼる

翌6日、家族と一緒に平和公園で催された原爆投下10年の慰霊祭へ行った禎子ちゃんは途中、歯ぐきから出血したと、急きょ病院に戻ってきました。

　ところがその一泊の間に禎子ちゃんは「あの歌を覚えてきた」と言うのです。メロディーも歌詞もしっかり覚えていて私に教えてくれました。

　その後の人生で何度も歌うこの歌は、たどればここから始まったのです。

原爆を許すまじ

浅田石二 作詞
木下航二 作曲

ゆっくり感情こめて

ふるさとの まちやかれ みよ りのほねうめし やけつちに
いまはしろいは な さーく あー ゆるすまじ げんばくを み
たび ゆるすまじ げんばくを われらのまちー に

(株)音楽センター　提供

Never Again the Atomic Bomb

1. *Our hometown was burned to the ground*
   We buried our family's ashes under the hot soil
   Now white flowers are blooming
   Oh, never again the Atomic Bomb
   We must never allow a third one on our hometown

2. *Our hometown's sea was stormy*
   After the black rain, we had no joyful days
   Now there are no people on their ships
   Oh, never again the Atomic Bomb
   We must never allow a third one on our Seto Inland Sea

3. *Our hometown's sky is heavy and dark*
   Black clouds cover the grounds again today
   Now there's no sunshine from the sky
   Oh, never again the Atomic Bomb
   We must never allow a third one in our sky

4. *Brothers and sisters had worked very hard*
   Finally they'd won fortune and happiness
   Now they've lost all fortune and happiness
   Oh, never again the Atomic Bomb
   We must never allow a third one on our Earth

Lyrics by Ishiji Ishida
Composed by Koji Kinoshita

原爆を許すまじ

一、ふるさとの街やかれ
　　身よりの骨うめし焼土(やけつち)に
　　今は白い花咲く
　　ああ許すまじ原爆を
　　三度(みたび)許すまじ原爆をわれらの街に

二、ふるさとの海荒れて
　　黒き雨喜びの日はなく
　　今は舟に人もなし
　　ああ許すまじ原爆を
　　三度許すまじ原爆をわれらの海に

三、ふるさとの空重く
　　黒き雲今日も大地をおおい
　　今は空に陽(ひ)もささず
　　ああ許すまじ原爆を
　　三度許すまじ原爆をわれらの空に

四、はらからのたえまなき
　　労働にきずきあぐ富と幸(さち)
　　今はすべてついえさらん
　　ああ許すまじ原爆を
　　三度許すまじ原爆を世界の上に

日本音楽著作権協会(出)許諾第 0512745-501

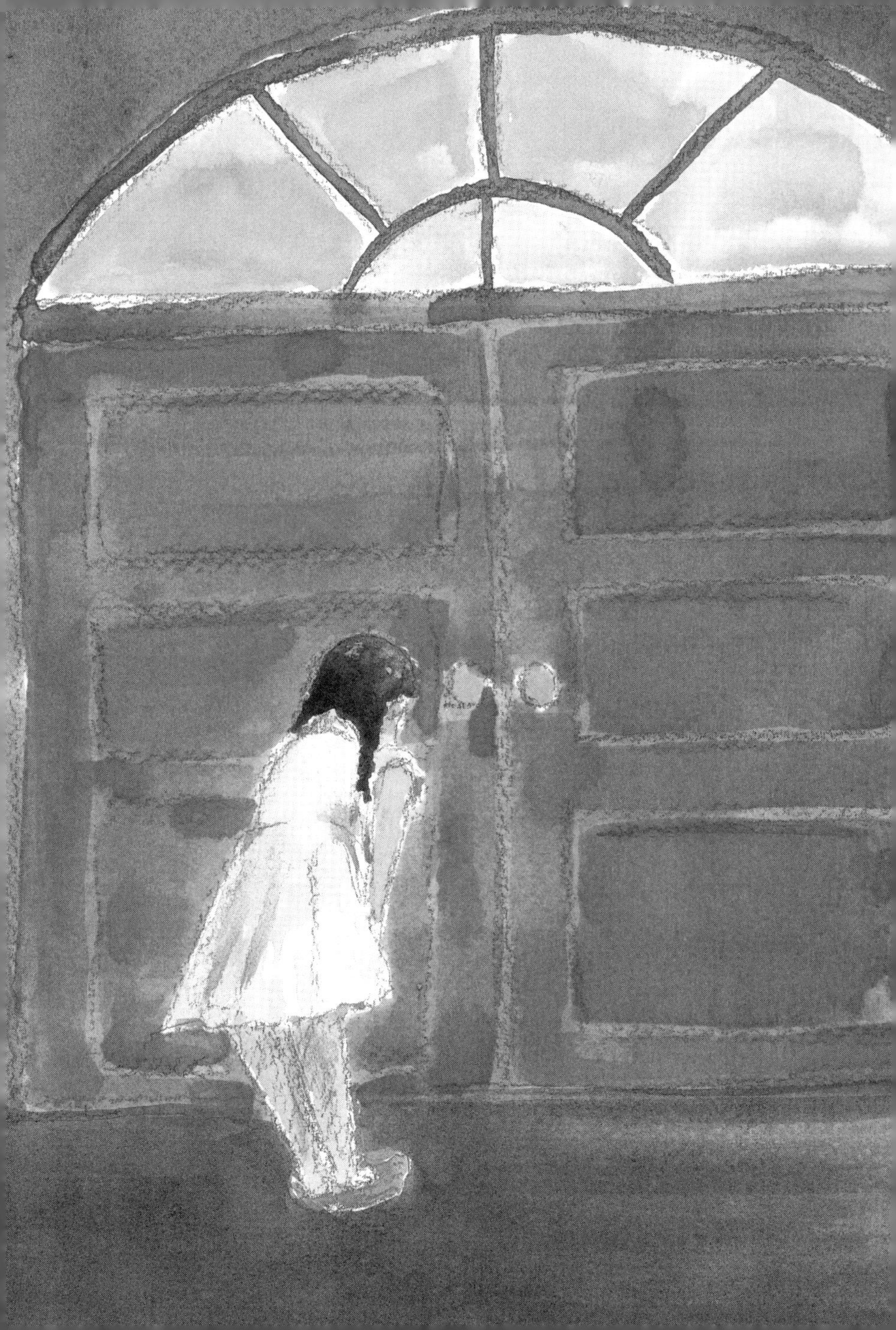

Chapter 6

One Thousand Paper Cranes

千羽鶴

Chapter 6

The paper cranes that put Sadako on the path to becoming a world-famous A-bomb victim after her death arrived as a present sent by high school girls in Nagoya "to patients with A-bomb disease" at the Hiroshima Red Cross Hospital. Sadako received some of the cranes. A perceptive girl like Sadako certainly made the connection. Sadako had an idea. The beautiful string of cellophane cranes she received was shiny and fascinating. "Why don't we make our own?" In those days, it was not easy to get *origami* paper. We didn't want to make cranes with white paper, like the paper our medicine came in. We began collecting wrapping paper. It wasn't easy. Not many sweets wrapped in pretty paper came from visitors to children who were hospitalized for a long time. Sadako leapt into action.

Word

- **crane** 名 鶴
- **victim** 名 被害者
- **perceptive** 形 察しのよい
- **string** 名 数珠つなぎになったもの
- **cellophane** 名 セロファン
- **fascinating** 形 魅力的な
- **leapt** 動 leap（さっと動く）の過去・過去分詞

One Thousand Paper Cranes　千羽鶴

　後にサダコを有名にしていく「折り鶴」は、名古屋の高校生から「原爆症の患者さんに」と送られてきたのを禎子ちゃんももらったことがきっかけでした。当時病院は、禎子ちゃんに原爆症である事を隠していたようですが、同じ病室でも自分だけがもらい、内科に行ってももらった人はすぐ分かる。賢い彼女のことですからきっと感づいていたことでしょう。セロファンで折られた鶴の房はきらきらと魅力的でした。「ウチらも折ってみようか」ということになったものの、当時は今のように折り紙がたやすく手に入る時代ではなく、身近にある薬の紙は白くて面白くない。

| Chapter 6

She walked around the hospital collecting wrapping paper. When we got some, we cut strips 30 centimeters in width. We folded and cut these into four equal strips. Starting with one corner of the strip, we folded a series of triangles. Then we cut out the squares formed by two of these triangles. The many small squares we made this way went into a box. Our squares were the same size as the small *origami* paper available today. Such small cranes as these, we could fold easily in the air, lying on our backs.

Beautiful, colorful wrapping paper like we see today was not available at that time. Most wrapping paper had some kind of pattern on a white background. When we were working with squares that contained only a bit of the pattern, we made sure that the pattern part showed. Sadako especially enjoyed thinking up ways to make our paper cranes as beautiful as possible.

Word

- **strip** 名 切れはし
- **fold** 動 折る
- **square** 名 正方形
- **in the air** 空中で
- **back** 名 背中
- **contain** 動 ～を含む

One Thousand Paper Cranes　千羽鶴

　私たちは包装紙を集めるところから始めました。と言っても長期入院の子どもの部屋にそうそう包装紙につつまれた見舞品がくるわけもなく、ここでも彼女の行動力がものを言いました。病院中を回って集めてきた紙をまず30センチ巾に切り、それを4等分して出来た短冊を端から三角に折って、はさみで切り、箱に溜めておきます。この大きさはいまの小さい折り紙と同じ大きさで寝たまま宙で折れるのです。

　包装紙といっても現在のように洒落たカラフルなものは少なくたいていは白地に同じ模様がちりばめられているものが多く、短冊にした時、白い部分が目立つと、私たちはいかに模様の色を取り込むかを工夫したものです。特に禎子ちゃんはそういう工夫を楽しんでいました。

| *Chapter 6*

As we folded, a competition grew between us. Soon, we were folding even during rest time and after lights-out. Nurses began to scold us, so we agreed not to fold at those times. We inpatients had nothing much to do, so it took us only about two weeks to make a thousand cranes each.

The Sadako legend holds that she continued to fold paper cranes with all her heart, hoping for recovery, but in vain.

I know that after I left the hospital, her condition grew steadily worse. That was when she made those tiny paper cranes displayed in the Radiation Effects section of the Hiroshima Peace Memorial Museum. I imagine her folding them compulsively, like the legend says.

Word

- **competition** 名 競争
- **lights-out** 名 消灯時刻
- **scold** 動 叱る
- **inpatient** 名 入院患者
- **legend** 名 伝説
- **in vain** （苦労などの）かいなく
- **radiation effect** 放射線の影響
- **compulsively** 副 衝動的に

二人で折ると競争みたいになって、安静時間も消灯時間も折っていてよく看護婦さんに叱られました。そこで協定を結んだりもしたのですが、他にすることのない病院生活２週間くらいで千羽はすぐに折れてしまいました。

　サダコ伝説では、病気の回復を願って一羽一羽心を込めて折っていたがついに力尽きて……ということになっているようですが。

　たしかに私が退院した後病状が悪化していく中で、あの資料館にあるような小さな鶴を折っている時、きっと彼女は必死だったと思います。

| Chapter 6

Fear must have seized her often, even when she was folding paper cranes with me. But at that time, I only saw the surface. I didn't see her anxiety. Rather, we talked about trivial things. Our chats about this and that, the songs we hummed, all these became precious, pleasant memories.

We did not keep our 1000 paper cranes in bunches like the movies or book illustrations about Sadako suggest. We each strung our cranes on one long thread that we draped in loops on our curtain rails.

I don't know why different versions are told about the number of the paper cranes Sadako folded. Each time moviemakers or writers consulted me, I told them that Sadako and I each folded 1000 paper cranes.

Word

- □ **seize** 動 ～を襲う
- □ **anxiety** 名 不安
- □ **trivial** 形 ささいな
- □ **hum** 動 鼻歌を歌う
- □ **precious** 形 貴重な
- □ **bunch** 名 房
- □ **strung** 動 string (～ひとつなぎにする) の過去・過去分詞
- □ **drape** 動 垂らしてかける
- □ **consult** 動 (専門家などに) 質問する

One Thousand Paper Cranes 千羽鶴

　私と一緒に折っている時もきっと心の奥底には不安がいっぱいあったことでしょう。でも当時の私は表面しか見ていなくて、それに気づくことなくむしろ日々の他愛ない会話をし、鼻歌を歌いながら過ごしたあの時間は穏やかな楽しい思い出として残っているのです。

　折り上がった鶴は映画や本の挿絵に見られるような房ではなく一本のひものように長くつなぎ、カーテンレールにループ状に飾りました。

　鶴の数もなぜか諸説生まれています。映画や本になる時、私たちはそれぞれ千羽折りましたと話しているのですが……。

| Chapter 6

After I left hospital, she resumed folding paper cranes. Perhaps that's why the story went about that "Sadako didn't make it to 1000 paper cranes."

Word

□ **resume** 動 再び始める

あの後、彼女はもう一度折り始めたので、それが「千羽に届かず……」ということになったのかもしれません。

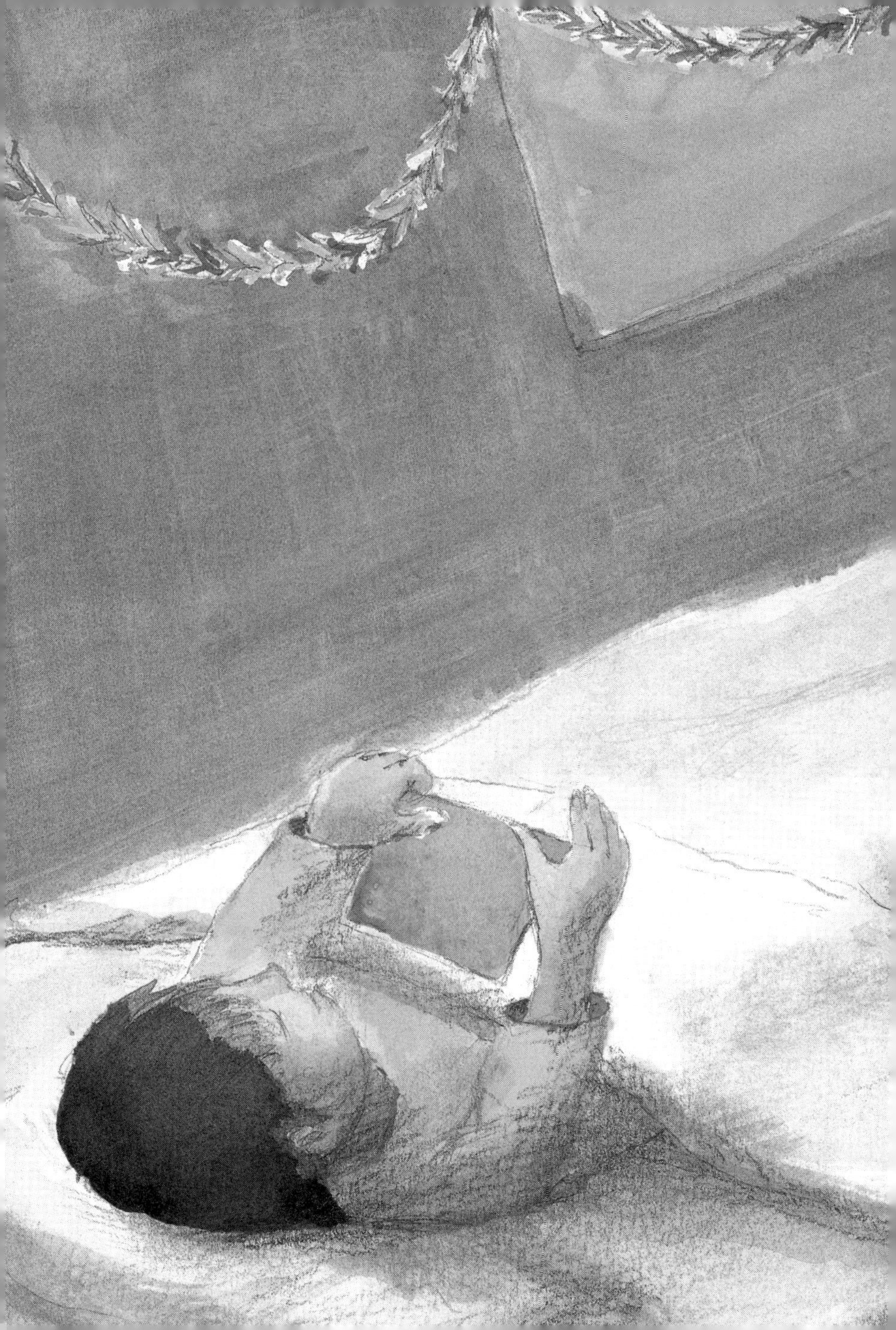

Chapter 7

Entering Adolescence

思春期の入り口に立つ

Chapter 7

Now that I'm a full-fledged adult, I can look back on my childhood. I remember a day I stood at the threshold to my own adolescence.

I was at school when the song *Yuki no Furumachi wo* (A Town Where It Snows) by Hideo Koh came over a loudspeaker to tell us it was time to go home. I suddenly felt something come over me. For no particular reason, my heart was racing. It was almost time for our graduation ceremony from elementary school.

Through a town where it snows
Through that town where it snows
Nothing but memories pass. . . .

Word

- **full-fledged** 形 成熟した
- **threshold** 名 入り口
- **come over** 〜が胸に去来する
- **race** 動 ドキドキする
- **graduation ceremony** 卒業式
- **nothing but** 〜だけ

Entering Adolescence　思春期の入り口に立つ

　大人になり、子ども時代が見えるようになって気がついたことですが、私には自分が思春期の入り口に立ったのはあの日だったと思えることがあります。

　小学校の卒業式も近いころ下校放送の音楽で高英男の歌う『雪の降る町を』が流れてきた時突然、何故かいつもと違って胸の奥がざわめいてドキドキしたのです。

雪の降る町を、雪の降る町を
思い出だけが通り過ぎて行く
………

| Chapter 7

I believe that was the moment I entered adolescence. I never asked Sadako about her moment, but I feel that she entered adolescence one summer day when we were together. I had been observing subtle signs that she was standing at the threshold. Later on, when I realized that I was the only one close enough that summer to perceive subtle signs of a transition that echoed my own, my love for Sadako deepened.

I was reading a book one day when Sadako said, "I'm thinking about reading a book." At that time, there were no novels for teenagers, though a few magazines for teens were appearing. We were trying to read novels in paperback to broaden ourselves. We wanted to act like adults. A grownup friend had influenced me to try reading novels that were somewhat beyond me.

Word

- **observe** 動 ～を観察する
- **subtle** 形 かすかな
- **perceive** 動 ～に気づく
- **transition** 名 変遷
- **broaden** 動 （範囲などを）拡げる
- **act** 動 振る舞う
- **beyond** 前 ～の理解力をこえた

あの瞬間が、私の思春期の入り口に立った時だったのではないかと思います。禎子ちゃんの胸のうちを聞いたわけではないけれど、この夏の日のどこかで禎子ちゃんも思春期の入り口に立ったのではないでしょうか。そのかすかな気配を私だけが見ていたと思うとわが事のそれと重なり、愛しさがこみ上げてきます。

　ある時、本を読んでいる私に「ウチも読んでみようかな」と言ってきたのです。当時は未だジュニア小説の分野の本はなく雑誌が数種類出始めた頃で、私たちは大人の読む文庫本を背伸びして読んでいた時代でした。私も早熟な友人の影響で、よく理解も出来ないのに読んだ気分になっていたのですが……。

| Chapter 7

Sadako started reading *Gan* (*Wild Goose*) by Mori Ogai. It was the thinnest of the three Ogai books then sold in a pocketbook set. She must have skipped over the Chinese characters she didn't know. She later reacted to *Gan*: "Tama is a very sad woman. I want to visit Muen-zaka when I visit Tokyo someday."

One day I said to her, "I'm going to write a letter to the Pen Pal Seekers section in this magazine. How about you? Do you want to?"

"Sure. I'll send a letter too!" She put her information on a postcard and sent it off. The magazine connected her to someone she didn't know, and the two began corresponding.

Word

- **goose** 名 雁《鳥》
- **Chinese character** 漢字
- **pen pal** 文通友達
- **seeker** 名 希求者
- **send ~ off** ～を発送する
- **correspond** 動 文通する

禎子ちゃんはたまたま私の手元にあった３冊の文庫本の中から一番薄い森鷗外の「雁」を手にしました。きっと漢字などは飛ばして読んだのでしょうが「お玉はかわいそうなんだね」とか「いつか東京へ行ったら無縁坂にも行ってみたいね」と感想を言っていました。

　また私が「雑誌の『おたよりちょうだいコーナー』にハガキを出すけれどあなたもやってみる？」と言うと

　「うん、やる！」と言って自分でハガキを書き、やがて見知らぬ人との文通も始めました。

| Chapter 7

In later years, I moved to Tokyo and visited the National Diet Library.

When I found our names in the magazine, good memories came back and tears ran down my cheeks.

On summer evenings, Sadako and I used to play tag and or hide-and-seek with the younger children on the roof of the hospital. After the children went back to their rooms, I loved to gaze at starlight brightening in the twilight. It was an adolescent thrill. At first, Sadako would leave with the children, saying, "I'm hungry." In time, she began to remain on the roof after the kids left, drawing contemplative sighs with me.

Word

- **National Diet Library** 国立国会図書館
- **play tag** 鬼ごっこをする
- **hide-and-seek** 名 かくれんぼ
- **roof** 名 屋上
- **gaze** 動 注視する
- **twilight** 名 たそがれどき
- **adolescent** 形 思春期の
- **thrill** 名 心がぞくぞくする感じ
- **contemplative** 形 物思いにふける

後年上京して、国会図書館で二人の名前の載った雑誌を見つけたときは懐かしさに涙があふれました。

　夏の日の夕方には、よく小さい子たちと屋上で鬼ごっこやかくれんぼなどして遊びました。子ども達が部屋に引き上げた後も、思春期真っ只中の私は黄昏ていく空に星が輝きを増すのをぼんやり眺めているのが好きでした。初めのうちは「お腹が空いた！」と子ども達と引き上げていた禎子ちゃんがいつの間にか隣りに立ち、一緒にため息をつくようになっていました。

| Chapter 7

We communed in a sweet silence. We were growing up. If Sadako had lived a little longer she might have written about her fears and desires like Anne Frank did. I cannot restrain my fury about A-bomb disease cutting off her bright future when she was so young and fresh.

Word

- commune 動 心を交わす
- restrain 動 〜を抑制する
- fury 名 激怒
- A-bomb disease 原爆病

言葉を交わすことなく二人それぞれの思いでたたずんだあの甘やかな空気は確かに思春期だったのです。そのように少しずつ心のひだが、増えていた時でした。もう少し長く生きていたら禎子ちゃんもアンネ・フランクのように心の叫びを記し、残していただろうと思うと命の瑞々しさを断ち切られた悔しさと憤りを禁じえません。

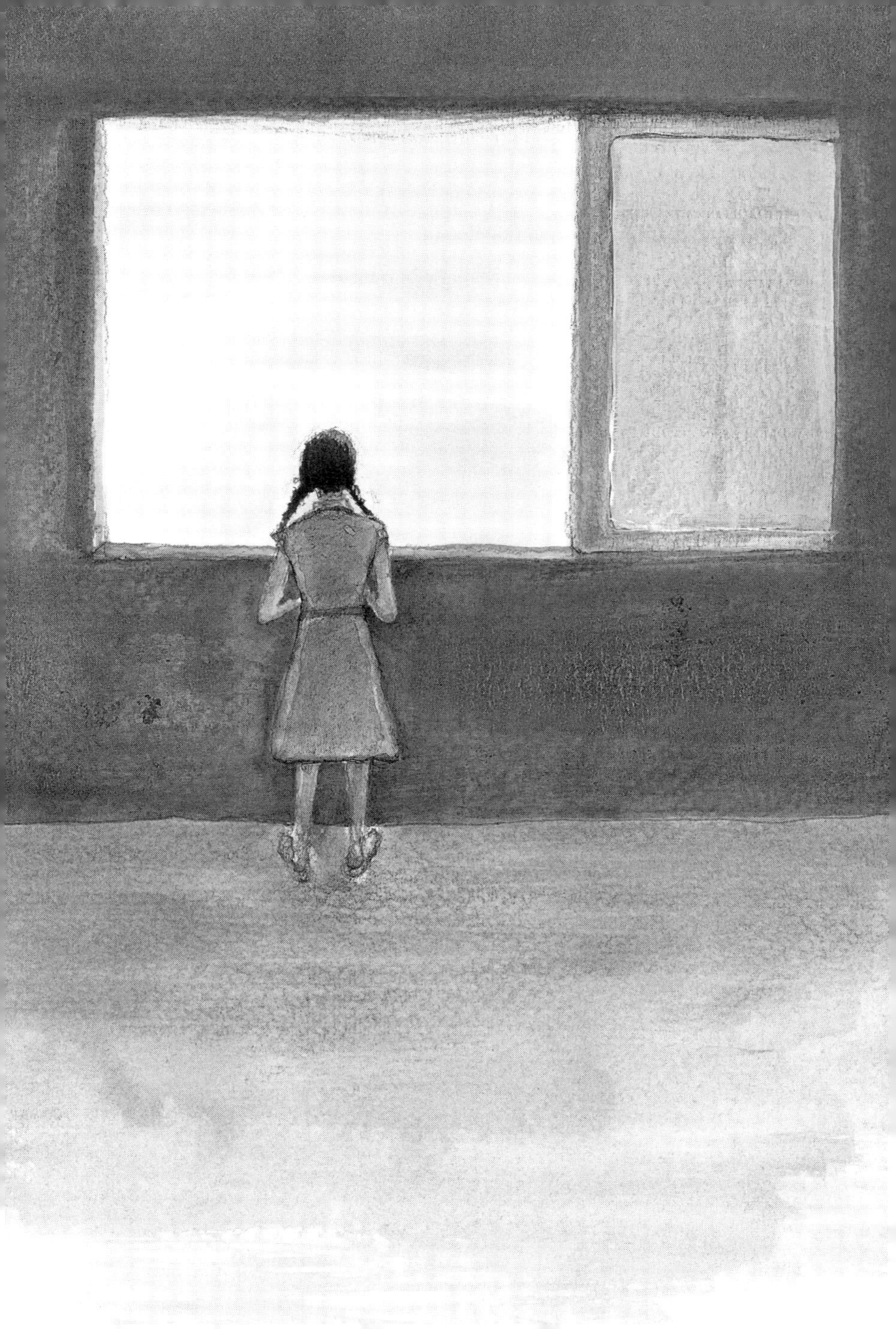

Chapter 8

To the Starry Heavens
星空へ

Chapter 8

After leaving the hospital, I recuperated with my family in the countryside.

Since my family was too poor to subscribe to a newspaper, I learned about Sadako's death from a newspaper article sent a week later by my relatives in Hiroshima City.

I had heard that Sadako was getting worse and worse the autumn after I left hospital, but I never imagined that this turn for the worse would lead to her death.

I was stunned!

Even after learning about her death, I failed to imagine the pain and fear she must have suffered as she was dying in her bed. The first thing that came to mind was our experience

Word

- **recuperate** 動 健康を取り戻す
- **subscribe** 動 定期購読する
- **relative** 名 親戚
- **stun** 動 呆然とさせる
- **suffer** 動 苦しむ

退院後、田舎で療養していた私は当時貧しくて新聞をとっていなかったこともあり、禎子ちゃんの死を知ったのは市内の親戚が送ってくれた1週間遅れの新聞記事でした。

　秋に入り急速に症状が悪化してきていることは聞いていましたが、まさかそれが「死」に結びつくとは……。私にとって禎子ちゃんの「死」はそれほど遠いものでした。

　絶句！

　それを知っても、私は死に至る禎子ちゃんの苦痛や恐怖も想像できず、まず心に浮かんだのは、ゆきちゃんの死のあと、一緒にゆきちゃんの星を探したように、禎子ちゃんも星になっちゃった！　という

| *Chapter 8*

together after little Yuki's death. Sadako and I had looked for Yuki's star in the sky together. Now Sadako had turned into a star like Yuki-chan.

In my mind I heard Sadako's radiant voice squealing with delight as we watched the fireworks of Sumiyoshi Shrine together from the hospital roof.

On August 5th the following year, I visited Sadako's family with a thousand paper cranes that I had folded with a guilty conscience. I could finally accept Sadako's death.

Word

- **turn into** 〜に変わる
- **radiant** 形 晴れやかな
- **squeal** 動 歓声を上げる
- **shrine** 名 神社
- **guilty conscience** 罪の意識

想いと、病院の屋上で住吉さん（住吉神社）の花火をみんなで見た夜の晴れやかな禎子ちゃんの声でした。

そして翌年の8月5日、時間とともにつのる自責の念をこめて折った千羽鶴を持って佐々木家を訪ね、初めてその死を受け入れることができたのです。

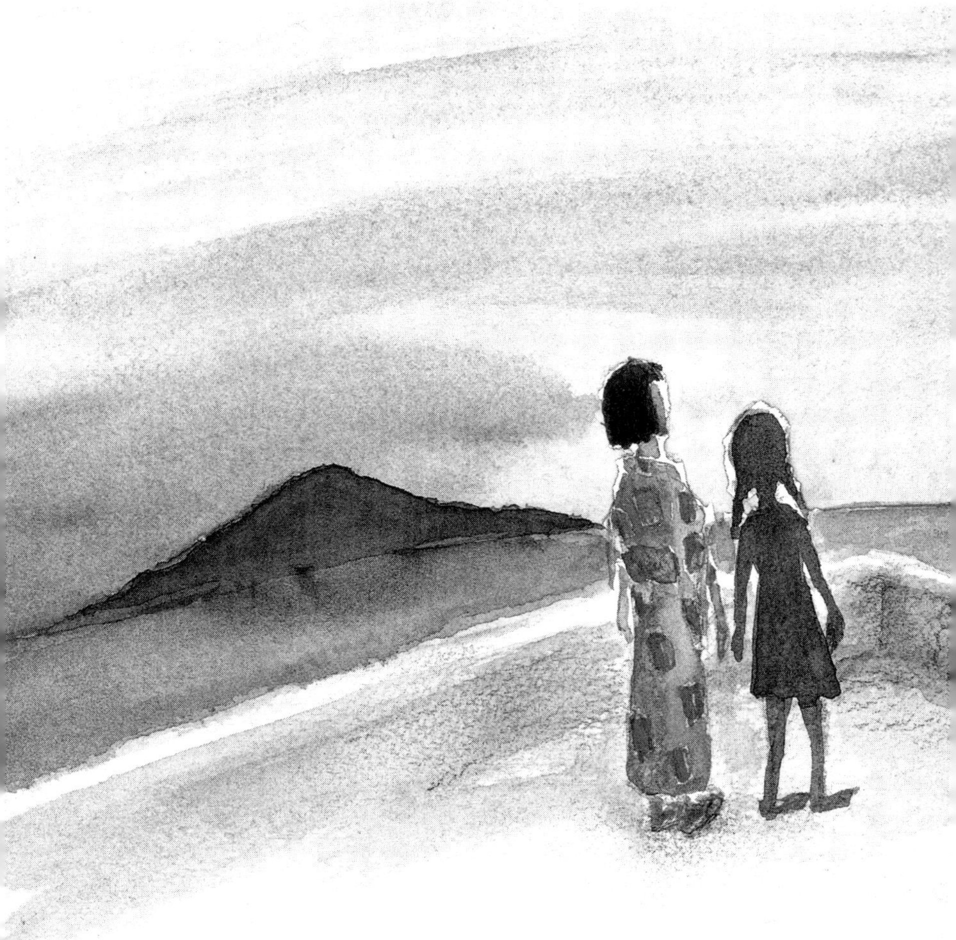

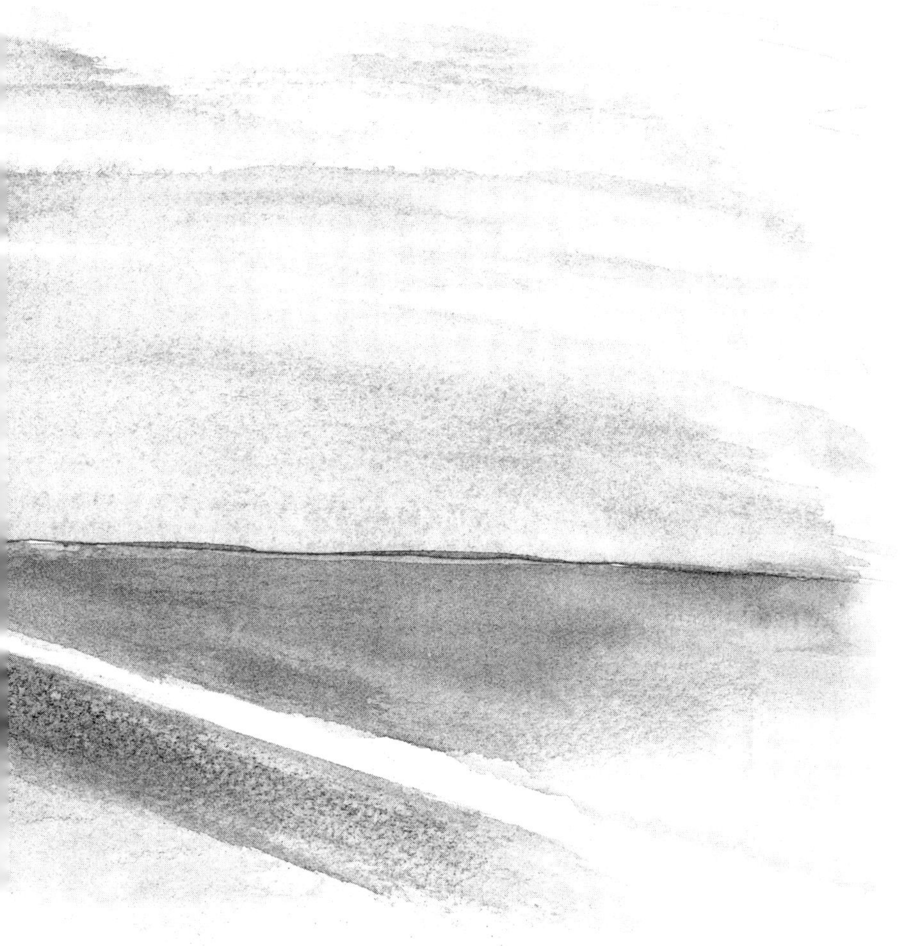

Epilogue

I have rarely talked about my relationship with Sadako. Though I was a child when I knew her, I always felt I had given Sadako too little consideration, done too little for her. As "Sadako and her thousand paper cranes" became a global peace symbol attracting ever more attention, I suffered from excessive media exposure simply for having lived with her at the hospital.

Ten years after her exposure to the radiation of the atomic bomb, scars appeared on Sadako's skin. Ten years after the Hiroshima bombing, Sadako suffered and died from A-bomb disease. At that time, there were no institutions or treatments for the mental and physical scars from the A-bomb. What pain and despair would seize anyone diagnosed with A-bomb disease!

Though I was only 14, I regretted not having the maturity to empathize deeply with Sadako's situation. Whenever

その後

　私は自ら進んでサダコとの関係を言うことはほとんどありません。それは、子ども時代のことだったとはいえ、禎子ちゃんのおかれた立場も理解出来ず、何もしてあげられなかったという思いをずっと抱いて生きてきたからです。彼女と折り鶴が世界平和のシンボルとクローズアップされる過程で、私はただ一緒にいたというだけで引っ張り出されるのは苦痛でした。

　被爆後10年も経って表れた放射能禍。また被爆者施策もない時代、薬も治療方法も無い中、「原爆症」と診断されたことは、本人もご家族にも絶望に等しいものだったことでしょう。

　その痛みを、14歳にもなっていながら、何一つ感じ取ることができなかった自分の、未熟さというより無知が恥ずかしく、禎子ちゃ

talking about Sadako revealed my immaturity and ignorance, I felt ashamed, chagrinned.

Given the important role that Sadako plays for world peace, I can't continue to hide behind an unwillingness to talk about her. I am mature enough to recognize my responsibility to convey the brilliance of Sadako's short life by sharing stories that show how she perched on the cusp of adolescence.

They say that the death of someone close changes our view of life significantly. Sadako's death changed my view of the peace movement because her death overlapped with my own family's A-bomb experiences. I cannot be indifferent to nuclear weapons. In my job and way of life, I have tried to commit myself to building lasting world peace without nuclear weapons.

んを語ることは、そうした自分をさらけ出すことでもあり、苦痛だったのです。

　しかし「サダコ」は今や、世界平和のために大きな役割を果たす存在になっています。私も自分の感情にばかりとらわれているわけにもいかず、私が語ることで、思春期という人生の大きな節目に立った禎子ちゃんの、短かった命の輝きを感じとってもらえるなら、それらを生きて味わった私の責務かなと思えるようになりました。

　「死」は人を育てると言いますが、私は思春期に禎子ちゃんの「死」と出会ったことで、自分や家族の被爆体験も重なり、戦争・平和への動きから目を放せなく生きてきました。特に核兵器には無関心ではいられません。この年まで、仕事や生き方を通し反核平和への気持ちは育ててきたつもりです。

Last October, I attended a memorial service for A-bomb victims at Noboricho Junior High School, the school Sadako dearly wanted to attend but never did. Instead of delivering my own message, I brought a message from Mr. Maki Sato of Japan International Volunteer Center (JVC). I wanted the Japanese children to know that Iraqi children know about Sadako.

When Mr. Sato delivered medicine to Iraqi children with leukemia to cheer them up, he asked them to draw self-portraits or pictures of their dreams. He has held exhibitions of their pictures all over Japan. One day, I read in the newspaper about an exhibition of Iraqi children's pictures called *SADAKO* and rushed to the exhibition hall.

Some drawings showed *Sadako* hooked up to a drip in bed. Some placed paper cranes next to *Sadako*. I was surprised that

昨年10月、禎子ちゃんがとうとう一度もいけなかった母校幟町中学の慰霊祭に、私は自分のメッセージの代わりに、日本国際ボランティアセンター（JVC）の佐藤真紀さんからのメッセージを橋渡ししました。それはイラクの子どもたちもサダコを知っていますよと伝えたかったからです。

　佐藤さんは、JVCでイラクの白血病の子どもたちに薬を届ける活動の中で、子どもたちを励ます意味を込めて自画像や、将来の夢などを絵に描いてもらい、日本各地でその絵の展示会をなさっています。ある時その紹介の新聞記事に「サダコ」というタイトルの絵があることを知り、私はその会場に飛んでいきました。

　ベッドに横たわり点滴を受けているサダコ、傍らに折り鶴も描かれている数枚の絵（実際にはもっとたくさんあるそうです）。イラク

*Sadak*o was depicted more than any other image. Why was *Sadako* getting so much attention in the far away, unknown world of Iraq? Eventually, I learned that the children had seen a movie entitled *Semba-Zuru (A Thousand Paper Cranes)* by Seijiro Koyama. This project is described in a booklet called *Kodomotachi no Iraq (The Children's Iraq)* published by Iwanami Shoten.

Nowadays, many Japanese know from television that Iraqi children are suffering from leukemia caused by the use of depleted uranium weapons during the Persian Gulf War 14 years ago (1991). But it feels to them like a distant story that merely provokes sympathy for something occurring in an entirely different dimension. I helped introduce drawings of *Sadako* by Iraqi children to Noboricho Junior High School students to show them that children are suffering right now the way *Sadako* did.

という未知の世界でどうしてサダコなの？という衝撃でした。子どもたちは映画「千羽づる」（神山征二郎監督）を観て描いたということでした。（このことは岩波ブックレット「子どもたちのイラク」に書かれています）

　14年前の湾岸戦争のとき使用された劣化ウラン弾が原因と言われるイラクの白血病の子どもたちのことはよく報道されますが、日本人にはまだまだ遠い国の話のようで、そんな子どもたちへの同情と、イラク戦争を止めさせる行動が、ともすれば別次元の話で終わってしまうのどかさには、いろんな角度から現実を知ることが大事ではないかと思い、「サダコ」の絵を紹介したのです。

I want them not only to recall Sadako Sasaki, but also to become aware of the *Sadakos* in their own generation. I call on them to cooperate with others to take a small step for peace.

Guided by the idea of "praying for peace with action," I've been taking my own small steps. I wish to help *Sadako*, a key bridge joining children all over the world, to protect the future for those children.

そしてサダコを思い出すだけでなく、同時代に生きているサダコとどう向き合うかを考えてほしい。そしてその事のために小さな一歩をみんなで踏み出そう、と呼びかけました。

　私自身、「平和への祈りを行動に！」この言葉を胸に、これからもサダコに架け橋になってもらって、子どもたちの未来を守る活動をしていきたいと思っています。

Afterword

It's been sixty years since the war ended. Everything seems to be at turning points, moving in new directions. I, too, need to make a step forward. Responding to various eager requests, I finally decided to write what I remember about Sadako. I had written one story about her for the last booklet in a series printed by a small association of A-bomb survivors. I had written another for the bulletin of a community education organization. I thought I had completed my mission to write a full account for all who wanted to learn more about Sadako.

However, I soon received an unexpected request from Yomo Publishing Company. They wanted to publish the story of Sadako to encourage more people to read about her. For various reasons, I rejected their offer repeatedly. Then, a sensitive female editor made me change my mind. She inspired me to try to convey the blossoming of this girl standing at the doorway to adolescence.

あとがき

　戦後60年の今年は巷に様々な形の「区切り」があふれましたが、私も一つの区切りをつける意味で、求められるままに初めて自分で禎子ちゃんの想い出を書きました。一つは、小さな被爆者団体の冊子の最終刊号に、もう一つは地域の教育関係の機関紙に。「サダコの話を聞きたい！」と言いながら忙しくてそんな時間もとれない人たちに、後でゆっくり読んでもらえばいい、私はちゃんと話しましたよ、という思いがありました。これで区切り、終りにしたつもりでした。

　ところが突然よも出版の方から、本にしてもっと広く読んでもらおうという話が飛び込んできました。私自身全然その意志はないと固辞しつづけたものの、最後寄り切られたのは、思春期という人間開花の命の輝きを大切に思って下さった女性編集者の感性でした。

In truth, I was diagnosed this summer with cancer. After undergoing an operation, I suffered terrible pain as a side effect of an anticancer drug administered during the operation. I was in excruciating pain for 24 hours. When it ended, I felt exhausted and completely helpless. I considered abandoning the effort to revise and edit this text. Dizziness and pain prevented me from concentrating on what I was doing. I could never have published this story without the enthusiastic support of that editor.

I am still worried that this book will fail to attract readers, but at least I have taken it to the end. I finish with the hope that it will help people learn to appreciate adolescence, the time of blossoming possibilities.

September 20, 2005

Kiyo Okura

実は私はこの夏、突然ガンと名のつく病気と診断され、手術、抗ガン剤投与の副作用と、24時間の苦痛に、もう何も彼もどうでもいい無力感でいっぱいになりました。そんな中、推敲も加筆もままならず、何度も投げ出してしまいながらの原稿になりましたが、何とか形になったとしたら、それは編集者の熱意の表れです。私としては一読に耐えるものかどうか不安ですが、誰にも訪れる思春期、その命の開花、可能性いっぱいの時を自ら愛しいと感じてほしいと願いつつ閉じます。

　2005年9月

　　　　　　　　　　　　　　　　　　　　　　　　大倉 記代

Sadako and Kiyo

Ten years after the atomic bomb was dropped, Sadako and Kiyo were in the same hospital room. Sadako was 12 years old and Kiyo was 14. Kiyo was in the midst of adolescence while Sadako was on the cusp. Sadako and Kiyo began folding paper cranes. It was a friendly competition to reach 1000, but they were serious about their hopes for recovery.

In Japan, legend has it that if you fold one thousand paper cranes, your wish will be granted. After folding one thousand paper cranes in only two weeks, Kiyo was miraculously released from the hospital. It didn't happen for Sadako. Sadako said to Kiyo, "I'll fold another thousand." It was not until Kiyo had become an adult that she saw the tiny colorful cellophane paper cranes that Sadako had folded on her deathbed. She saw them displayed at the Hiroshima Peace Memorial Museum. After Kiyo left the hospital, Sadako's condition got worse, but she continued folding the tiny,

禎子ちゃんと記代さん

　原爆が投下されてから10年後、禎子ちゃんと記代さんは同じ病院に入院していました。禎子ちゃんは12歳、記代さんは14歳。記代さんは思春期の真っ只中、一方の禎子ちゃんは思春期の入り口に立っていました。二人は折り鶴を折り始めます。鶴が千羽になるまで折ることは楽しい競争でしたが、それには二人の回復への心からの願いが込められていました。

　日本では折り鶴を千羽折ると願いがかなう、と言われています。わずか2週間で千羽を折り終えて、記代さんは奇跡的に退院します。でも禎子ちゃんの退院はかないません。禎子ちゃんは記代さんに「もう千羽折るの」と告げるのでした。記代さんは、大人になって初めて禎子ちゃんが死の床で折っていた小さな、色とりどりのセロファンの折り鶴を目にしたのです。その小さな折り鶴は広島平和記念館に展示されています。記代さんの退院後、禎子ちゃんの病状は悪くなる一方でしたが、父親には「心配しないで。いい考えがあるの」と言って、小さな美しい紙の折り鶴を折り続けました。

beautiful paper cranes saying to her father, "Don't worry. I have a good plan."

No one knows why, but her paper cranes gradually became smaller and smaller. The last one was a tiny 2-millimeter red crane. Two months after Kiyo left hospital, Sadako passed away because of disease caused by the atomic bomb.

For fifty years, Kiyo never forgot Sadako. She continued quietly working for peace, hoping for a genuinely peaceful world without nuclear weapons and no more Sadakos, victims of war and radiation from nuclear weapons.

In 2005, Kiyo went to New York to participate in events surrounding a review conference on the Nuclear Nonproliferation Treaty (NPT). Soon after she came back to Japan, she discovered that she had ovarian cancer. It was in

なぜ禎子ちゃんの折り鶴がどんどん小さくなっていったのか、誰にもその理由は分かりません。最後のものは、わずか2ミリの赤い折り鶴でした。記代さんが退院して2か月後、禎子ちゃんは原爆が原因の病気で亡くなります。

　50年間というもの、記代さんは禎子ちゃんのことを忘れたことはありません。記代さんは、核兵器のない真の平和な世界、戦争と核兵器による放射能被害者である禎子ちゃんのような人を再び生まない世界をめざして、平和のために黙々と活動を続けました。

　2005年に、記代さんは核兵器不拡散条約（NPT）再検討会議に関連して開催されるイベントに参加するためにニューヨークに赴きます。帰国後間もなくして、卵巣ガンが発見されます。記代さんは、ガン病棟の病室で『想い出のサダコ』を書き上げます。

her room on the Cancer Ward that she finished her memoir for publication.

Her book was published on October 25th in 2005, commemorating the 50th anniversary of Sadako's death. On February 25th of 2006, Kiyo launched the "Sadako-Rainbow Fund" with her two friends, Atsuko Moriya and Keiko Miyamoto to help Iraqi children suffering from radiation-caused leukemia like Sadako. They were dying due to the effects of depleted-uranium munitions. Until her death on June 23rd 2008, Kiyo devoted all her energy to the "Sadako-Rainbow Fund". After Kiyo's death, artist Kentarou Yokawa stepped in as head of the "Sadako-Rainbow Fund" to carry out Kiyo's wishes. Like Sadako, Kiyo folded paper cranes until the moment of her death.

その本は、禎子ちゃんの死後50年を記念して2005年10月25日に出版されました。2006年2月25日、記代さんは、禎子ちゃんのように放射能が原因の白血病で苦しむイラクの子どもたちを救おうと、友人の守屋敦子さんと宮本慶子さんと「サダコ」・虹基金を設立します。イラクの子どもたちには使用済みウラン廃棄物のせいで死の危険が迫っていました。2008年6月23日、記代さんは亡くなる日まで、「サダコ」・虹基金に全精力を傾けていました。記代さんの死後、画家の夜川けんたろう氏が代表に就任し、記代さんの遺志を受け継いでいます。記代さんは、禎子ちゃんのように亡くなるその時まで、折り鶴を折り続けていたのです。

About Sadako

The day the atomic bomb was dropped, two-year-old Sadako was in her mother's arms. Sadako had no external wounds or burns, and grew to be a healthy girl. She was good at all kinds of sports. She especially loved running. She could run much faster than the boys. She was a very popular girl in her class, and was always the anchor in relay races.

When she was about 12 years old and looking forward to being a junior high school student, she fell ill and, suspected of having leukemia, was hospitalized. Eventually, the diagnosis of "A-bomb disease" was confirmed.

Sadako never went to junior high school. She passed away on October 25th 1955. On her hospital room curtain rail hung the one thousand paper cranes she had folded. At her bedside were some half-folded cranes. All those cranes watched fondly over Sadako as she passed away.

禎子ちゃんについて

　原爆が投下された日、2歳の禎子ちゃんは母親に抱かれていました。禎子ちゃんは原爆で怪我も火傷も負わず、すくすくと育っていきます。運動は万能でした。なかでも走るのが得意で、男の子たちですら禎子ちゃんに勝つことはできないほどでした。クラスの人気者で、リレー競走ではいつもアンカーをつとめました。

　12歳になって中学校にあがろうとしていたとき、禎子ちゃんは病に倒れ、白血病の疑いで入院し、最終的に原爆病と診断されたのです。

　禎子ちゃんが中学校に通うことはありませんでした。1955年10月25日、禎子ちゃんは身罷ります。病室のカーテンレールには、禎子ちゃんが折った千羽鶴がかかっていました。ベッドの脇には、折りかけの鶴が残されていました。これらの鶴は、この世から去っていく禎子ちゃんを愛おしげに見つめていました。

Her classmates, students in Noboricho Elementary School, were shocked and saddened by Sadako's sudden death. They wanted to do something for her, so they began raising funds to build her a monument. This eventually became the campaign that resulted in the Children's Peace Monument, one of the most popular monuments in Peace Memorial Park.

The Children's Peace Movement moved teachers and, eventually, the Japan Association of School Principals. The money raised came from more than 3,000 Japanese schools and even from the UK and other countries overseas.

The Children's Peace Monument was unveiled on May 5th, 1958. At the top of the tower stands a statue of Sadako holding a golden paper crane. Under the monument, an inscription reads, "This is our cry, this is our prayer, for

禎子ちゃんの突然の死に、禎子ちゃんが通っていた幟町小学校の児童たちはショックを受け、悲しみました。そして禎子ちゃんのために何かしたいと思いたち、記念碑設立の募金を始めます。この募金の結果として、平和記念公園に、一番有名な記念碑の一つ、「原爆の子の像」が設立されたのです。

　この「広島平和をきずく児童・生徒の会」の運動は教師たちはもとより全日本中学校長会をも動かしました。募金は、3,000を超える日本中の学校、さらには英国をはじめとする海外諸国からも寄せられました。

　「原爆の子の像」は、1958年5月5日に公開されました。台の上には金色の折り鶴を持つ禎子ちゃんが立っています。像の下の碑には「これはぼくらの叫びです　これは私たちの祈りです　世界に平和をきずくための」という言葉が刻まれています。

building peace in the world."

In fiscal 2009, about 1.4 million people visited the Hiroshima Peace Memorial Museum in the Peace Park. Every year over ten tons of paper cranes (more than ten million cranes) are sent from children all over the world to the "Children's Peace Monument".

2009年度には、140万人ほどの人が平和記念公園の広島平和記念館を訪れました。毎年、世界中の子どもたちから、10トン以上の折り鶴（1千万羽以上の折り鶴）が「原爆の子の像」に届けられています。

About Kiyo Okura

Kiyo Okura was born in Hiroshima in 1941. When she was four, she was exposed to the atomic bomb 3.3 kilometers from the hypocenter. Kiyo and her mother hurried to an air-raid shelter covering their heads with a *futon*(quilt). That *futon* was dotted with stains of radioactive black rain. In December 1954, she was hospitalized at the Hiroshima Red Cross Hospital. In June 1955, Sadako became Kiyo's hospital roommate. Later, Kiyo moved to Tokyo and became a high school librarian.

Kiyo passed away in Tokyo in June 2008.

大倉記代さんについて

　1941年広島県生まれ。4歳の時、爆心地より3.3キロの地点で被爆。母親と2人、夏掛けを頭に被って防空壕に向かう。夏掛けには黒い雨の跡が点々とあったという。1954年12月、肺浸潤で広島日赤病院に入院。翌年6月、禎子と同室となる。8月末退院。その後、上京し高等学校図書館司書となる。

　　　　　　　　　　　　　　　　　　2008年6月、東京にて逝去。

Photo by K. Yokawa 撮影：夜川けんたろう

Courtesy of Kiyo Okura　写真提供：大倉記代氏

Sadako (Left), Kiyo (Right)　病院にて。禎子（左）と記代

Sadako In the World

August 6	1945	An atomic bomb was dropped on Hiroshima. Sadako was 2 years old.
February	1955	Sadako was diagnosed with leukemia.
October 25	1955	Sadako passed away at the age of 12.
	1956	Jewish journalist Robert Jungk came to Japan.
	1958	Robert Jungk published *Children of the Ashes*.
May 5	1958	The Children's Peace Monument was unveiled.
	1961	An Austrian writer of children's stories, Karl Bruckner, published *Sadako will leben*. The book was translated into 22 languages and read by more than two million people.

世界中で愛されるサダコ

1945年 8月6日	サダコが2歳のときに、広島に原爆が投下される。
1955年 2月	サダコが白血病と診断される。
1955年 10月25日	サダコ、12歳で逝去。
1956年	ユダヤ人のジャーナリスト、ロバート・ジュンク氏来日。
1958年	ロバート・ジュンク氏 Children of the Ashes 出版。
1958年 5月5日	「原爆の子の像」が公開される。
1961年	オーストリアの児童文学作家カルル・ブルックナー氏が『サダコは生きる』を上梓。本書は22ヶ国語に翻訳され、200万人以上の人たちに読み継がれている。

	1968	In Barcelona, Spain, a "Sadako School" was founded.
	1977	A Canadian author, Eleanor Coerr, published *SADAKO*.
	1993	The peace animation *On a Paper Crane* was created by Miho Cibot-Shimma. (Director and Screenplay by Arihara Seiji) It has been shown in more than 65 countries around the world. It was shown at the UN in 1995.
August 6	1995	Children from Los Alamos, New Mexico, where the Hiroshima and Nagasaki bombs were made, built the "Children's Peace Statue" now located in the garden of the Albuquerque Municipal Museum.
September 21	2013	An exhibit honoring Sadako was unveiled at the Pearl Harbor Visitor Center on Oahu, Hawaii, featuring a photograph of Sadako and one of the paper cranes she folded.

1968年	スペインのバルセロナに「サダコ学校」が創設される。
1977年	カナダ人の絵本作家エレノア・コアが『サダコと千羽鶴』を上梓。
1993年	有原誠治監督・脚本によるアニメーション「つるにのって　とも子の冒険」が制作され、世界65ヶ国以上で上映される。1995年に国連でも上映。
1995年　8月6日	広島と長崎に投下された原爆がつくられたアメリカのニューメキシコ州ロスアラモスの子どもたちが「子どもたちの平和の像」を制作。現在、アルバカーキ市美術館の庭園に設置されている。
2013年　9月21日	ハワイのオアフ島パール・ハーバーのビジター・センターにサダコのコーナーが設置され、サダコの写真とサダコの折った折鶴が展示される。

本文DTP　ドルフィン
ナレーター　Deirdre Merrell-Ikeda
録音スタジオ　株式会社 巧芸創作

大倉 記代 *Okura Kiyo*

1941年広島県生まれ。4歳の時、爆心地より3.3キロの地点で被爆。母親と2人、夏掛けを頭に被って防空壕に向かう。夏掛けには黒い雨の跡が点々とあったという。1954年12月、肺浸潤で広島日赤病院に入院。翌年6月、禎子と同室となる。8月末退院。その後、上京し高等学校図書館司書となる。2008年6月、東京にて逝去。

夜川 けんたろう *Yokawa Kentarou*

画家。1968年東京生まれ。日大芸術学部美術学科卒。1993年イタリア・ベネツィア美術アカデミア入学。1996年ベネツィア・アトリエ・アペルト版画工房に移る。イタリア・日本での個展多数。『あの日　見たこと』、『小さな木の実ノート』（よも出版刊）などで装幀、挿絵を手がける。

想い出のサダコ

2015年7月10日　第1刷発行

著　者　大倉 記代

発行者　浦　晋亮

発行所　IBCパブリッシング株式会社
　　　　〒162-0804 東京都新宿区中里町29番3号 菱秀神楽坂ビル9F
　　　　Tel. 03-3513-4511　Fax. 03-3513-4512
　　　　www.ibcpub.co.jp

印刷所　株式会社 シナノパブリッシングプレス

© Kiyo Okura 2005
© Yomo Publishing Ltd. 2010
© IBC Publishing Inc. 2015

Printed in Japan

落丁本・乱丁本は、小社宛にお送りください。送料小社負担にてお取り替えいたします。
本書の無断複写(コピー)は著作権法上での例外を除き禁じられています。

ISBN978-4-7946-0353-1